WEST CORNWALL in the OLD DAYS

Douglas Williams

Stories and Photographs that Span a Century

BOSSINEY BOOKS

First published in 1985
by Bossiney Books
St Teath, Bodmin, Cornwall.
Printed and bound in Great Britain by
A. Wheaton & Co. Ltd, Exeter.

ISBN 0 948158 08 5

To my wife Jane

FRONT COVER: St Ives, by courtesy of The Royal Institution of Cornwall, coloured by Paul Honeywill.
BACK COVER: surveying the damage to the old promenade at Penzance.

About the Author and the Book

Douglas Williams, who has always lived and worked in West Cornwall, has his home at Newlyn, the fishing town where he was born.

Married, with two daughters, he has been a local journalist for over thirty years, and knows West Cornwall, its places and its people, from his own personal involvement in the area, and from his family background here.

Music and drama are among his leisure interests, and he has sung with operatic and choral societies throughout Cornwall. The Rotary Club movement and the Methodist Church also play an important part in his life. A Bard of the Cornish Gorsedd, his Bardic name sums up his interests, 'Voice and Pen'.

In 1984 he made his debut for Bossiney with *Mount's Bay* in which he took readers on a journey — in words and pictures — from Land's End to Lizard Light.

Of *West Cornwall in the Old Days*, he writes: 'The strength of West Cornwall lies in its enchanting variety. Every corner and cove, village and stream, harbour and hill, has its power to appeal.

'The Saints of St Just, St Buryan and St Ives, the old boroughs of Penzance, Marazion and Helston: all have their individual personalities.

'The ports of Newlyn, Porthleven, and Hayle, the havens of Lamorna, Sennen, Mullion and Porthgwarra, all linked by this enormous coastline, are as separate in identity as they are in attraction.

'The moorlands and crofts, the stark granite cliffs and sweeping pastureland, the hedges, the flora, unchanged for generations, speak of continuity and security.

'The sea is never very far away in West Cornwall: there is almost an island splendour here.'

We have deliberately included some modern photographs to show that old traditions are sustained here in West Cornwall.

An Island Splendour

The strength of West Cornwall lies in its enchanting variety. Every corner and cove, village and stream, harbour and hill, has its power to appeal.

The Saints of St Just, St Buryan and St Ives, the old boroughs of Penzance, Marazion and Helston: all have their individual personalities.

The ports of Newlyn, Porthleven and Hayle, the havens of Lamorna, Sennen, Mullion and Porthgwarra, all linked by this enormous coastline, are as separate in identity as they are in attraction.

The moorlands and crofts, the stark granite cliffs and sweeping pastureland, the hedges, the flora, unchanged for generations, speak of continuity and security.

Left: Flower time in the Boskenna and Penberth districts and no shortage of work. The flowers were in 'beds' rather than single rows, and the daffodils, picked in bloom — not in bud as today — were placed in jars and steamed dry so they would have a long life for the buyer.
Right: Baskets by the dozen, and the catch is checked on the beach, with the Mount's Bay fleet just offshore.

Right: A happy 1950 beach view of St Michael's Mount from Marazion beach; ideal for any tourist brochure.

Below: In January 1952 the Liberian steamer *Liberty* went ashore under Pendeen lighthouse, and here the breeches buoy is in action. The St Just Lifesaving Association rescued 22 of the crew during the night, and 13 others were brought ashore in the morning.

Right: **A delightful quiet corner of St Ives (at Barnoon Hill) with the parish church in the background, photographed in about 1901.**

The sea is never very far away in West Cornwall: there is almost an island spendour here.

The grandeur of Land's End and Zennor, the charm of Mousehole, Perranuthnoe and so many of the little hamlets, the rugged character of Cape Cornwall and Pendeen, the history of Godolphin, Paul and Prussia.

A sunrise over the castle of St Michael's Mount, a sunset over the Longships Lighthouse. The sounds of the sea, and the gulls calling. The colours and the scents of bluebells and gorse, heather and primroses.

This is our abiding heritage and culture. It is as it has always been: in turn magnificent and fascinating, spectacular and mysterious.

This is my theme. United though West Cornwall may be in administration, and indivisible in Celtic spirit, each town and village has its own personal pride, its own ceremonies and traditions. We are their guardians. Too much has already been lost, too many Feasts almost abandoned, too many legends forgotten. Our generation has a mighty task to ensure these flourish, despite the lures of contemporary society, the dramatic changes in population, and ever-increasing tides of sophistication.

Below: **Anybody going to St Just — sorry but we are full up! The coach is at the bottom of Church Road in Pendeen, 'Richard Warren's bus'.**

Those Fabulous Fish

The West Cornwall fishermen finished their celebrations to mark the end of the pilchard season, and stood for the traditional toast:

Here's a health to the Pope,
May he live to repent,
And add just six months
To the term of his Lent.
It's always declared
Between the two poles,
There's nothing like pilchards
For saving their souls!

These Cornish fishermen could see the ecumenical sense of it all. As Methodists they toiled at Newlyn, Mousehole, St Ives, Porthleven and Sennen to prepare their enormous hauls of pilchards for the Roman Catholics of Italy.

Today we associate too much romantic legend, and not enough of the unremitting strain and struggle to the trade.

When the corn is in the shock
Then the fish are on the rock,

was the couplet, and this pilchard season continued from August for many months.

There were the 'Huers', perched at strategic points, waiting to see the tell-tale signs, the fish leaping out of the water, the rush of bubbles to the surface, and the red-hued cloud under the water when the shoal was large. Up would go the cry of 'Heva' — a local call for 'Here they Are' — nowadays retained with the Heva Cake, which was made when there was a little money to spare.

The names of the Seine Companies were legion, from Good Intent to Speculation, real evocative names, and in 1827 there were 316 seines, with almost 3,000 men working them at sea, and over 60,000 on shore.

The 'Huer', with his furze bushes,

Above: When fishermen are not at sea there are always a hundred and one jobs to be done. These at Sennen are tarring the ropes, in 1924.

Left: In comparatively recent days the casks of pilchards went out from Newlyn pier by steamer to Italy. Here they are being loaded.

would give the semaphore-style signals to direct the boats precisely where to 'shoot' the quarter-mile long net.

There were fabulous catches. In 1868 one seine took 16½-million fish, and 150 years ago 10,000 hogshead, or 30-million fish were enclosed at St Ives within an hour!

It was not only the men who toiled. The women and girls, from teens to old age, worked in the cellars with the fish and the salt, putting the pilchards in layers until the pile was as high as their reach, twenty feet long and four feet broad. The fish overwhelmed the villages. Every boat, every court, every cellar — smoking, pickling and salting . . . Pilchard Palaces indeed. Mountains of them.

One Vicar remarked that the smell was sometimes so strong as to stop the town clock! The industrial spin-off was enormous, and today many a village and port has its 'Coopers Court' and its 'Ropewalk' as a reminder of those days.

The net was shot around the fish, which were trapped alive, the ends were closed and the net warped inshore with the aid of capstan and muscle. The flashing silver harvest was taken out of the seine by small tuck nets, and brought to harbour by little craft. Huge numbers escaped only to die and be washed ashore.

The old luggers made the bays of West Cornwall seem almost like the Sea of Galilee, with their age-old skills on fine summer nights, and a calm sea. In those days there was no fishing on Sunday: even the shoals had a day off!

The fishing villages still have the remains of their 'Palaces', where the catch was dry-cured in salt, pressed to get the oil, and then shipped in casks for ports such as Ancona, Naples, Venice and Vecchia. Mr Harry Matthews of the Agents, J. H. Bennetts, reminded me of the ship *Shelldrake* which came to Newlyn up until the early 1950s to take the casks to Leghorn and Genoa.

In my own youth I remember the pilchard 'driving' fleet in Mount's Bay, with the seagulls trailing in flocks, swooping and weaving to pick up any morsels from the boats which at times were down so low in the water you felt sure the sea would swamp the decks.

Newlyn has changed greatly since this mackerel season scene of 1901, before the building of the fish market, and offices. The pub — now the Swordfish — is a signpost to help identify the area.

Left: The huer's 'bushes' show the seine boat fishermen exactly where to shoot their net to enclose the fish. Here are the genuine bushes used on the cliffs at Gunwalloe as a signal.

Below: 'Tucking' pilchards from a seine. When the fish were trapped alive in the mesh they were removed by small tuck nets after being brought near to shore. The fish are alive-alive-oh.

Above: **As the fishermen of St Ives bait the lines, in serious mood, the cats keep a look-out for any tit-bits.**

Right: **Fish packing, ready for the markets of Britain. A regular sight in West Cornwall.**

They had their own terms for the catch: 'a last and a half' — 10,000 pilchards made a last — was an individual way of reckoning. In later years the seine was replaced by the conventional net. Mr Harry Blewett of Newlyn, who was at sea in 1933 in the Mousehole boat *Penzer*, told me that 100 pilchards for a 'jowster', a fish seller, would always be 126.

I well recall the fishermen 'barking' their nets, dipping in cutch to preserve and dye them, and then hanging them over the harbour rails. My grandfather used his cellar for this work even to the post-war years.

There are still drift net boats working along the Cornish coast, and even recently Mr Michael Hosking of Porthleven, on his 100-foot trawler *Silver Harvester*, helped in the revival of the fishery with catches of 250 tonnes.

The nets may change, and the huge shoals have disappeared, but one delight remains unaltered: marinated pilchards, cooked in a dish with vinegar and bay leaves, are as delicious as ever.

Right: Few fishing boats had such long records as *The Pioneer*, landing her catch.

Below: A stalwart group of fishermen, on board, early in this century. Second from the left, seated, is my grandfather Mr William Henry Williams, for many years associated with two fishing boats, *Girl Lilian* — named after his daughter — and *Peel Castle*.

Right: **Who will bid for some fine fish? The auction at Newlyn.**

Above: A fine fish at Crowlas.
Above right: Young and old, women and children, come along to watch the fish auction of skate and ray on the foreshore at St Ives. In the background is the ship chandler's and grocers.

Right: Cornish fishermen look the same, whatever the port. Here, complete with peaked caps, is a group at Porthleven.

A Pride in Tradition

Those centuries of community life, tightly-knit between families whose names still flourish in St Ives, have made this town one of the most cherished in Britain.

Whistler and Sickert may have 'wintered' here a century ago, the artists who followed may have given the town an international reputation, and the hundreds of thousands of tourists brought a new prosperity.

Right: **The little 'corner' shop in St Ives, with its row of bottles in the window, pictured in 1910, with Doble's Wall on the right.**

Below: **Times have changed down on the Wharf at St Ives! In 1900 the fishermen could watch boats and tide, underneath C. Stevens, boot and shoe manufacturer, and Quick's sail loft.**

Yet for my personal palette the genuine hues of St Ia — that Irish princess who brought Christianity here in the fifth century — lie in two ceremonies that the people still hold close to themselves, uncluttered by modern sponsorship techniques, and media 'hype'.

One is the annual Feast Monday celebration, and the other the unique John Knill ceremony, which falls in 1986.

The traditions of 'Fair Mo' may be lost today, but Feast, held on the nearest Sunday to 3 February, holds its delightful silver hurling ball contest between Uplong and Downlong. The ball must be returned to the Mayor at the Guildhall at noon to set the seal on the Monday.

Being part of an enlarged district has not taken anything away from the individuality of this town. One could suggest a few more anniversaries here — how about a Hain Day to mark the enormous contribution to the town of the steamship company founder, Sir Edward.

What about a Pilchard Feast to recall those great years when millions of the fish were harvested? Or a ceremony to commemorate that poor Mayor of the sixteenth century, John Payne, who was tricked into having his own gallows built?

John Knill was a Collector of Customs . . . but it was claimed he was in league with the smugglers. He erected a mausoleum, with a hollow sarcophagus for his remains . . . but was buried in London. He was born in Callington . . .

Below and left: That famous silver ball. On Feast Monday in 1985 the St Ives Mayor, Mr J.B.Thomas, prepares to throw the silver ball to the crowds of youngsters waiting on the beach.

but was St Ives' most colourful personality.

His 50-foot high granite 'Knill Steeple' is the stage for a ceremony once every five years, such as 1981 and 1986, on St James Day, 25 July. A fiddler leads ten little girls dressed in white, with two elderly widows, off from the town for a dance around the Steeple.

It all began in 1801 when Mr Knill, also responsible for the building of Smeaton's Pier, was present. An iron chest, with its three locks to keep the ceremony funds secure, still exists.

D. H. Lawrence, like Bertrand Russell and Dylan Thomas, knew the St Ives Bay and Mount's Bay coastlines well, and often came down across the moors from his Zennor home to the towns.

There could hardly be a more remote cottage than the one in which he and Frieda chose to make their home. 'This strange looking couple' was a first impression Mr Stanley Hocking of St Ives gave to me, when he spoke about the couple's arrival there early in 1916.

He was about seventeen then, and his home was the nearby farmhouse. 'Law-

Below: **If any of these lads are alive today in St Ives they would be well into their nineties. The boy with his sailboat, the modest swimmer — all potential fishermen and mariners seen in 1901.**

Above: The little girls, all in white, and full of smiles, trip gaily around the Knill Steeple in St Ives' most delightful tradition. Then they pose with the fiddler, the Master of Ceremonies, and the two elderly widows. The first festival was in 1801.

rence wore long hair, a red beard, corduroy suit and a slouch hat: his wife was a very nice looking lady.'

Mr Hocking recommended Tregerthen, and within a week they had been to see the owner, Captain Short, and taken the cottage. 'In a place like Zennor, when strangers come amongst us people will usually start asking themselves, "Who are they?", and "Where do they come from?".

'Well, it didn't come out for a long time that Lawrence's wife was a German lady of very high standing — a cousin of Richthofen, the German air ace, and her father was a German Baron and high ranking officer in the German Army.

'Things were happening out at sea: it was nothing unusual to see two or three ships being torpedoed and sinking at one time.'

There were unfounded rumours that signals were being given from the shore to U. Boats. Feelings locally ran high, police searched the cottage in 1917, and they were told to leave this part of Cornwall. Soon they were back in London, never to return, but to leave some of the Cornish characters in Lawrence's novel *'Kangaroo'*.

Left: No holidaymakers about here! W. Rouncefield, fish merchant, is in business on the right, along the quay at St Ives.

Below: Another view of the sea front, this time in 1910, with the sailing ship, and the washing out to dry, while the boys make merry in the punts.

Right: These attractive young women are members of the staff of Honey's flourishing knitwear factory at St Ives, which at one time had over 70 at work. Mr Thomas Honey opened the factory in Dove Street soon after the start of the First World War, after the founding of the firm in 1889. His grandsons, Cyril and Tom Honey, continue the retail business in the town, but manufacturing ended a few years ago.

Left: **The bowler-hatted men of St Ives watch anxiously as the flood of November 1894 roars past them at Lower Stennack. On the right are the Wesleyan chapel and school, while the advertisements on each side of the road tell of the merits of Hudsons and Sunlight soap. There had been heavy rain for days and when it reached its climax with this 'river' of water there was considerable damage. Homes were ruined . . . and boats were used in the streets to rescue stranded townspeople.**

Right: The Sunday Schools of St Ives still parade with their banners on Whit Monday.

Below: A charming part of St Ives Mayor-making ceremony. The children drink from the traditional 'Loving Cup'. On the right are 1985 Mayor and Mayoress Mr and Mrs Mike Peters.

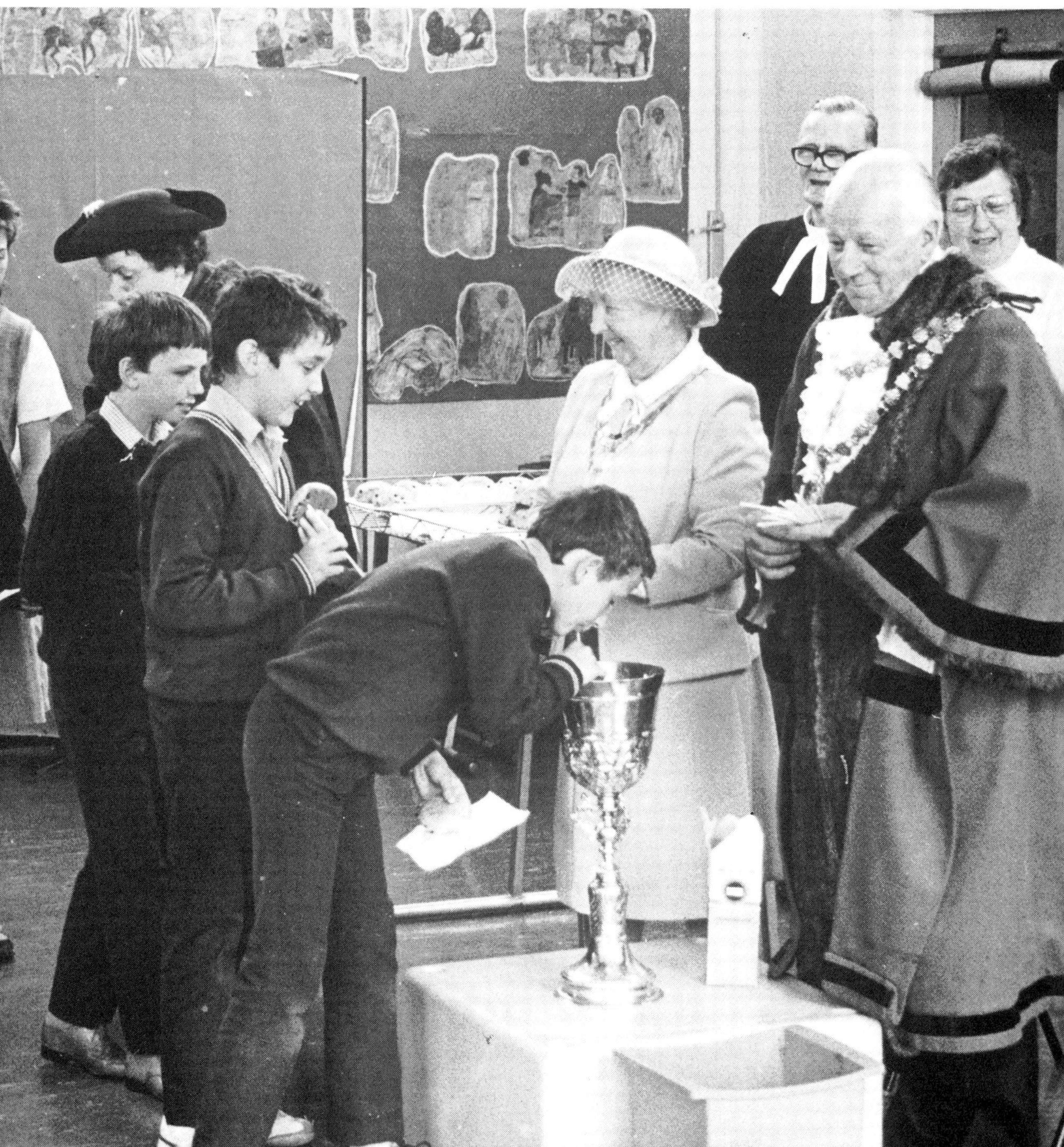

Guise dancing lives on in St Ives, as this contemporary picture proves.

Right: **The building of the St Erth to St Ives railway is under way. The 4½ mile line opened in 1877.**

Above: **It was in 1877 that the first steam engine passed over the full length from St Erth to St Ives, and the new railway was officially opened the following month. Today it is part of the 'Park and Ride' scheme after being saved from the Beeching 'axe', and still brings holidaymakers in thousands to the town. This picture of the station and Porthminster beach with its seine boats, was taken around 1900.**

All aboard the GWR bus at Marazion.

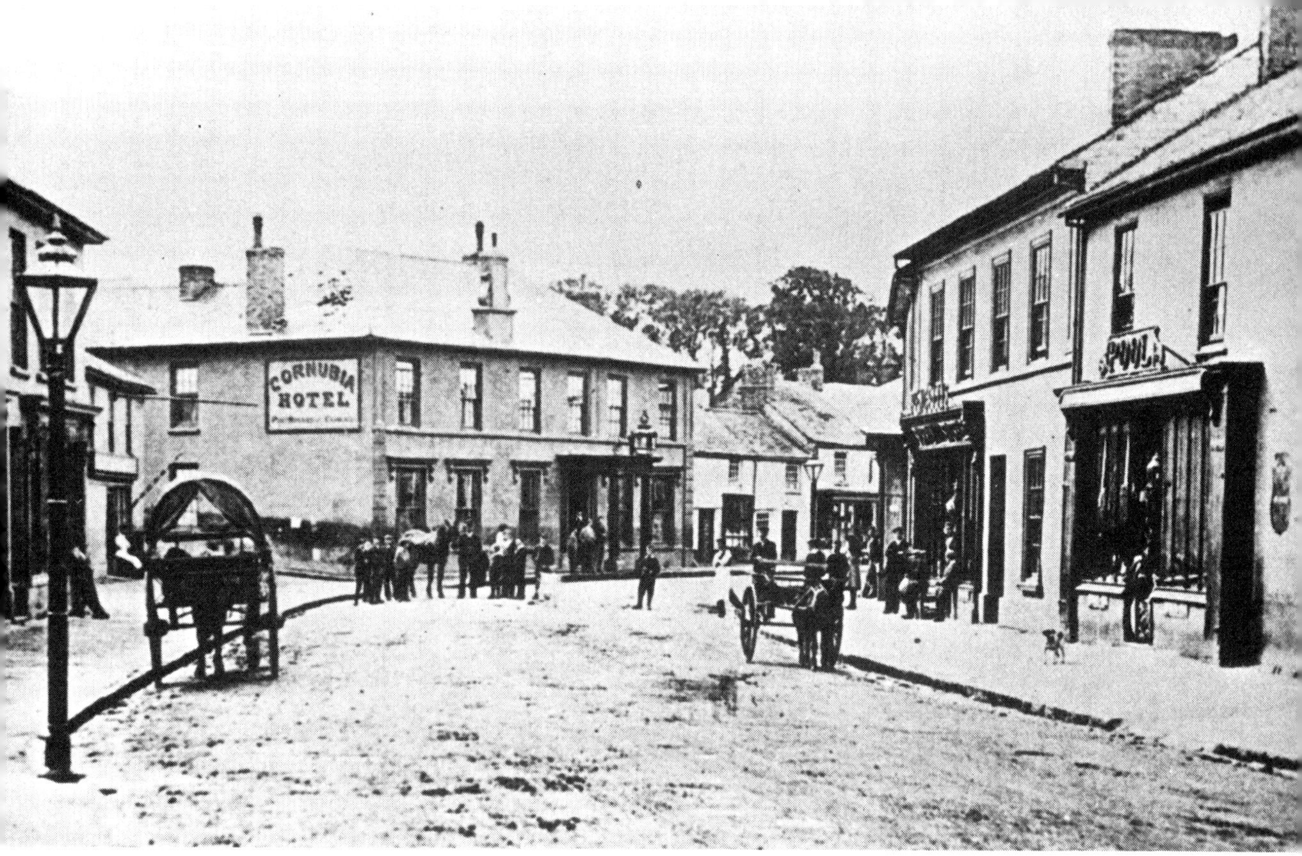
CORNUBIA
HOTEL
POOL

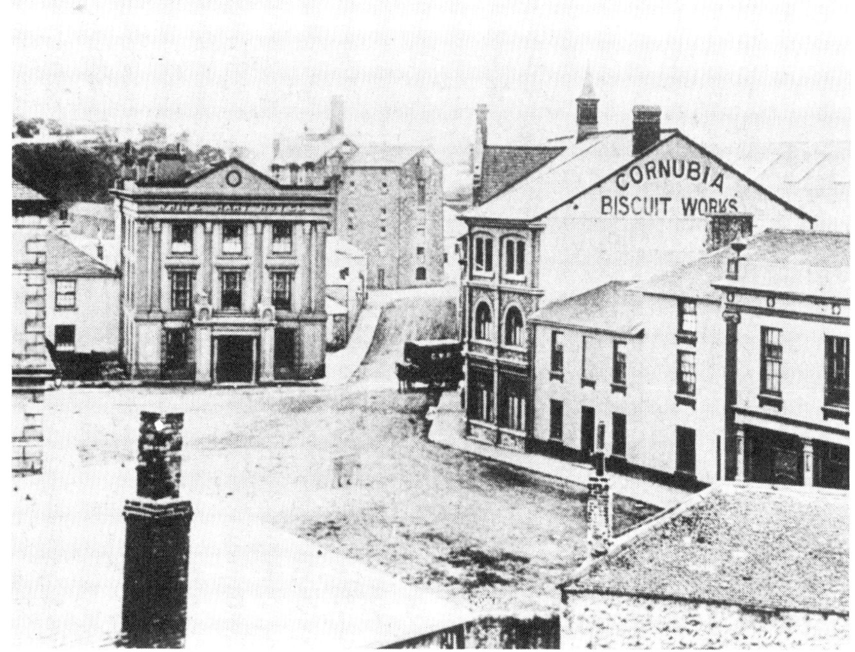

CORNUBIA
BISCUIT WORKS

Left: No tarmac road in Fore Street at Hayle in 1905. The pony looks after the transport, but the Cornubia Hotel is as imposing as ever.
Below left: The White Hart Hotel and many of these Hayle buildings remain with us, but not the Cornubia biscuit works and that horse-drawn GWR van . . . Foundry Square in 1910.

Hayle Regatta flourishes today as it did in these crowded days of September 1905, with all the town out to enjoy it.

Lucky 'Charms'

Although the local people, down the centuries, have been deeply religious, most fervent in their faith and evangelistic in their approach, they have never been short of superstitions.

In fishing villages around West Cornwall, filled with boats and chapels, 'warnings' and fears of tragedy abounded. It was a bad sign when a woman walked on a pier, and the word 'rabbit' was never used by a fisherman. Perhaps it came from the miners' belief that a rabbit's appearance in the engine house was a sign of a fatality.

I remember the Mousehole story of the fishermen with a new net. While putting it aboard the boat a woman stepped over it. The men looked at the skipper and said: 'You will never see that net any more.' And they never did: that night a steamer went over the nets, and that one was cut off!

If you returned to your house to collect something you had forgotten it was wise

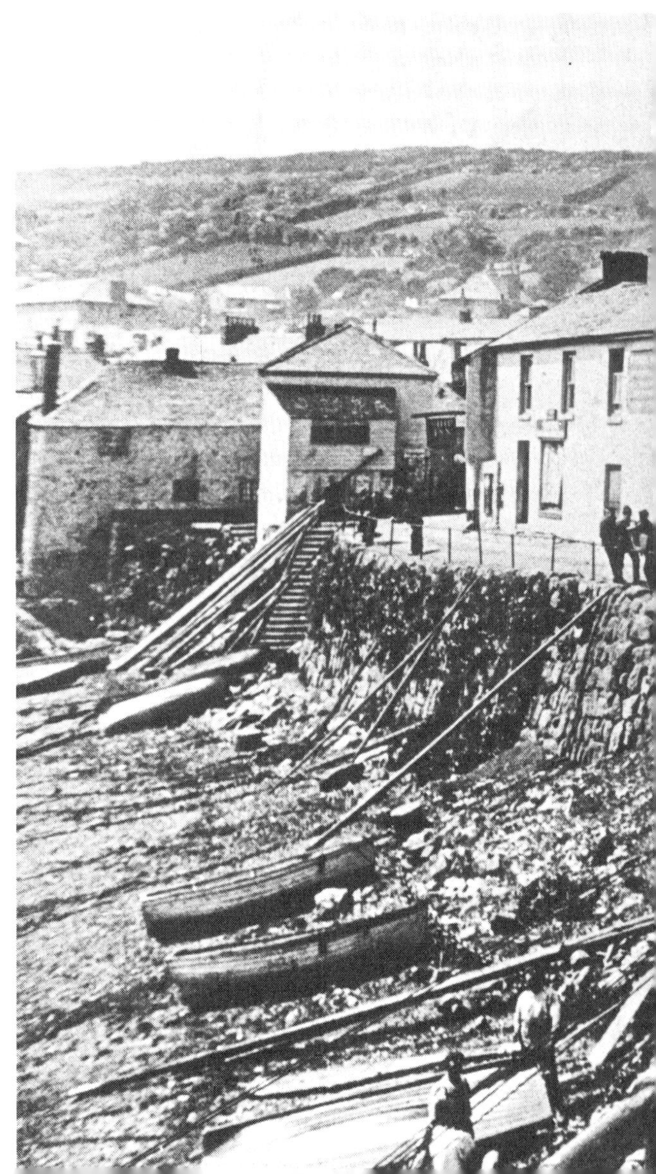

The fishing villages around West Cornwall have never been short of superstitions. Here in Mousehole care and vigilance has meant that the harbour front has remained unspoiled down the years. It seems only the traffic is missing!

Right: **A real Cornish tradition — a lad with his pasty.**

to walk three times around a chair beföre coming out.

Some fishermen believed that a pilchard should always be eaten from the tail towards the head, to bring good luck, and in the past century most villages had a character who could 'charm away' any warts on hands and face with a secret word, and a harbour-front spell. I recall an old fisherman who did this for me at Newlyn well over 40 years ago. I was so fascinated that I asked if he would pass the secret to me! I never learned where his magic went: perhaps the fact that his grandson became a local doctor put it all in perspective!

Below: **Never let a woman step over your net in West Cornwall. Here Smeaton's Pier at St Ives—started in 1767 and lengthened more than a century later—is the scene of net-mending in the 1930s. The fishermen are William Bennetts (right) and his father Edward: the grandfather and great-grandfather of present lifeboat mechanic Tom Cocking jnr.**

They Left Their Mark

It is so easy to overlook the contemporary scene when the history of a district is compiled. One firm at Penzance has spanned 150 years of industry and engineering in West Cornwall, in mining, farming, the home, and at sea.

The imprint of N. Holman and Sons has been an important one since its formation at St Just in 1834. It has not only made its mark, but also left its name.

Railings and lamp posts, manhole and hydrant covers still proclaim the Holman legend, owing their existence to the casting shops at the Penzance Wharf, and at Tregeseal Foundry. One-and-a-half centuries later, with Mr Anthony Holman as managing director, it continues its contribution to local prosperity.

That half-mile of massive railings at the promenade was first put in place from Battery Rocks to 'Public Baths' in 1896.

Those pre-war majestic cast iron railings at St John's Hall were made by Holmans. They were cut down for the 'war effort' in 1942 . . . but a large number of them were later sold back to Holmans at 30 shillings a hundredweight and cast for gratings and ploughs.

Their heads were of a remarkable design, and showed the craftsmanship of 'Ould Mathy Eddy'. He carved out a mahogany head to match the complex drawing, and then cut it into upwards of 40 pieces in such a way that the moulder could draw them out one by one. Finally the molten metal was poured into the cavity for an exact reproduction. Sadly the pattern was destroyed in the second World War bombing.

In 1873 the Gear Pole, just off Penzance, was made by Holmans for Trinity House. At St Just the first 'Cornish slab' was built, and revolutionised the cooking range design in the county. Today they

Left: **An evening tide, and the boats leave Penzance harbour for the night's fishing. A steamer's funnel, on the right, brings us into the twentieth century.**

may be collectors' items, but in their time they had a place not only in every home, but in every British lighthouse. It was also a reminder of home, for wherever the Cornish miner emigrated the 'slab' was not far behind!

Before Mr Nicholas Holman began his iron foundry at Tregeseal Valley the supplies for the mines were 'imported' from Hayle. But even in that first year of business a boiler, 20-feet long, and weighing 5¾ tons, went to the Portsmouth and Farrington water works costing £129. 7s 6d.

An immense amount was completed for the mines, from trams and pumps to pit head work, winding gear, and cages. But when this industry declined the attention was turned to farming. Pumping and irrigation machinery was designed and marketed. The first iron plough used in West Cornwall was made at the Penzance works.

As the years passed so the company moved into the cycle and motor-cycle and then the motor car business in Market Jew Street. And they even made those early 'velocipedes' at St Just.

It was not until 1904 that the present dry dock and the land around was bought at auction and gradually brought up to date, with major changes in the 1920s and 1930s in time for the centenary celebrations.

Down the years the Holman family continued in charge, including Nicholas

Below: **Fifteen horses are needed to pull this giant link with St Just's industrial past. This boiler is probably on its way to Levant mine. Holman's foundry at St Just played a great part in the life of this district.**

Holmans moved into the motor car business in Market Jew Street, Penzance. Here left, the first motor bus to leave Penzance for London on 30 September in 1919.
Below: **A scene in Market Jew Street during those years when the horse and the motorbus were in competition. On the right the 'Royal Mail' has arrived.**

The West Cornwall sanitary steam laundry at Penzance was a big employer over many years in New Street, with a large organisation. The ironing is under way.

jnr., William, John, Frederick, Walter, Edgar, Percy and in latter years, Selwyn.

Penzance became an auxiliary naval base in the First World War, and the offices became the headquarters of the Naval staff, with the whole of the output claimed by the Government for war purposes.

It was reported: 'The directors were conscious of the honour so conferred upon them, and proudly flew the Union Jack over the premises until the order to do so was countermanded by the War Office because the air raiders' attention was attracted to munitions factories by the flags, and so became objects of attack.' At St Just during this war 9-inch howitzer bombs were produced.

Not only were Cornish ranges being manufactured — and gaining awards — but more modern gas cookers were made for many years.

With war again in 1939 the Admiralty took over the dry docks, and gun parts were made at St Just. But in April 1941 the head office and stores at St Just were completely wiped out by three 100-pound bombs . . . production was only delayed for a week!

For many years the Penzance gas works was run by Holmans as agents for the Government, but in 1950 came nationalisation. The year 1954 saw the start of a revival at the dry dock and in the following years there was concentration of resources here, with the sale of the Market Jew Street car and motor-cycle premises, and the St Just garage.

Before the closure of the Foundry at St Just, in 1967, came a new clientèle, with the work of Dame Barbara Hepworth and several other sculptors being cast here.

The firm continues as part of the Penzance tradition, and even today there are thoughts of future development, and a proposal for a new dry dock in the harbour itself to allow easier access along the harbour road.

Left: Penzance promenade collapses under the 1880 storm. On the 'prom' itself is the former Lavin's Hotel, and the baths, while on the right can be seen Drew's Serpentine Works. This great Mount's Bay Storm on 7 October caused havoc with all seven fishermen on the Mousehole boat *Jane* being drowned, and some thirty fishing boats destroyed and sunk at their moorings. *Above:* Building work on the promenade, following the 1880 storm, with the giant pieces of granite being placed into position. On Ash Wednesday in 1962 came another destructive gale which resulted in the present promenade.

Above: September 1945 brought the first match for the new combined Penzance-Newlyn Rugby club. The home side, skippered by Peter Gartrell, went down 15–3 against Guy's Hospital . . . before a crowd of 3,000!

Left: Do you fancy a one-shilling evening trip on the RMS *Scillonian*? Here, in Penzance, the virtues of the 7.15 p.m. trip are proclaimed, plus the 'Trixie' Orchestra. They lived it up in those days.

Above: **Happy days for the Penzance Chapel Street Wesleyan Methodist Sunday School tea treat.**

Above: **General William Booth, with top hat and beard, in the centre of this Salvation Army group at Penzance — probably 1904.**

Mayors of Penzance. *Above:* All the huge crowd gives three cheers, with the Mayor standing at the top of the St John's Hall steps, with officials and councillors, and the soldiers below. It is 1901.

Right: During the Mayoralty of Alderman and Mrs Joseph Walter Meek (1932–34), the St Anthony Gardens were opened and the 'Jubilee' bathing pool — opened in 1936 — was inaugurated. They were both councillors, and Mr Meek, last Mayor of the old and first of the new borough in 1934, was presented with an illuminated address by the Council in appreciation of his efforts.

Above: Alderman George Ford, Mayor of Penzance 1951-53, leads this civic parade down Market Jew Street.

Below: The final days of the 'old borough' of Penzance, in 1974. Town Clerk Owen Wheale holds the 1614 Charter, with Mayor and Mayoress David and Margaret Pooley (left), and their deputies John and Beth Laity. Mr Pooley became first chairman of the new Penwith District Council.

Right: It was an historic day in September 1846 when the Royal yachts lay off St Michael's Mount, with Queen Victoria, Prince Albert, the Prince of Wales and the Princess Royal all gathered there. They 'honoured Mount's Bay with their presence', was the inscription on this engraving. An imprint of the Queen's foot was made on the steps where she landed from the Royal barge, Prince Albert played the church organ, and they went to the top of the tower to see St Michael's chair. One of the delightful stories in the Mount's history is the belief that the first of a newly-married couple to sit on this chair will gain the mastery in married life. We don't know which of the Royal partners was first to sit there!

Above: Queen Elizabeth the Queen Mother was a very popular visitor during the Mayoralty of Alderman Alfred Beckerleg (1964-66), and signed the visitors book in the Mayor's Parlour at Penzance.

Below: **Princess Anne took a great interest in the Chapel Street nautical museum of Roland Morris when she visited in May 1972. The Mayor Dr Jack Turney is with her . . . and the author on the right.**

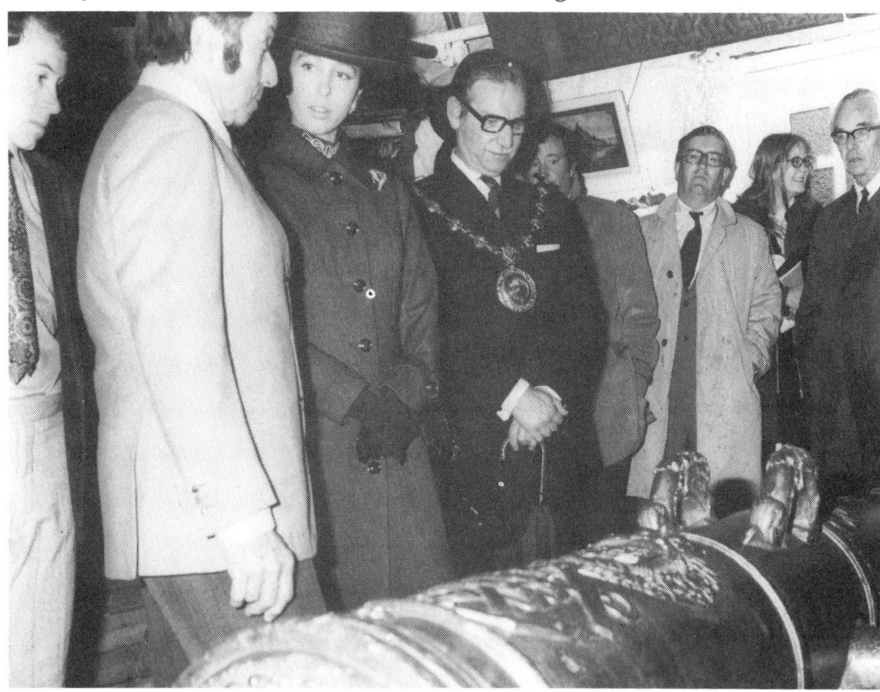

Murder Most Foul

The triple murder and suicide at Penzance in 1886 is rarely mentioned today, and little-known by the general public. No modern murder investigation would leave so many questions unanswered as did this tragedy which has possibly no equal in Cornish history during the past century.

It was a Wednesday lunchtime in July when, at Cottage Row, near the promenade, three were shot dead — two women and one man — and the murderer James Hawke then shot himself.

There was emotional involvement, and fierce upset, in the whole town.

Hawke even had time to reload the pistol during the slaughter. He killed his sister and brother-in-law, Mr and Mrs Uren, then he followed Mrs Gerrard, the wife of a jeweller, to the front door, and shot her.

Mr Gerrard ran and weaved from side to side, escaping the bullet aimed at him. Within a few minutes Hawke had shot himself.

The inquest was a curious affair, with only one of the two witnesses to the tragedy called to give evidence. He, Mr Gerrard, was vague and unconvincing, unable to explain what went on.

Several questions remained in the public mind. Did the witness tell the whole

truth? What started the row? Was it over a relationship between the murderer and his niece Clara?

There was equal controversy about the funeral: the crowd believed he should not lie at peace in consecrated ground, and chanted:

The parson will preach no sermon
The bell will never toll,
The ground receives his body,
May the devil receive his soul.

The riddle of the murders remains unanswered, and in 1972 Penzance lost possession of the murder weapon from the museum in Penlee House. It went to the police museum in Exeter, and all that is left in the home town is a photograph of that pistol.

Above: The gallant men of the Penzance Borough Force — every one with a moustache.

Below: The Chief Constable joins the Penzance policemen in this group.

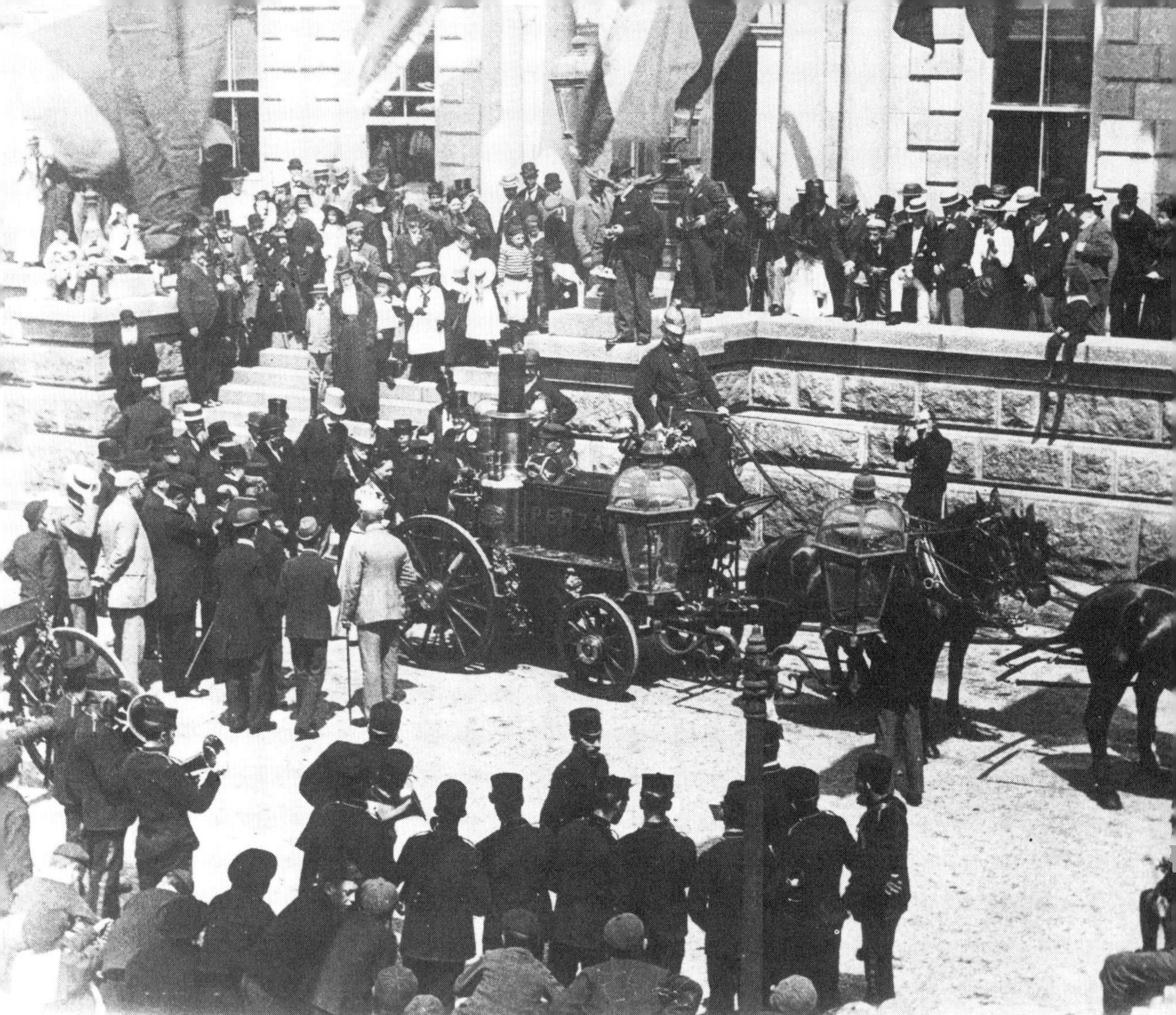

Above: A big day, with band, flags, and the Mayor, for the new Penzance steam fire engine, presented by Mr R.F. Bolitho of Ponsandane in 1895.

Right: It was in 1890 that a volunteer fire brigade was formed in St Ives, and here are the men at work in March 1915 at one of the most famous fires in the town, at Market Strand. Plenty of salt water to keep the hoses supplied.

Above: **There is pride in these war-time faces as they stand with their new Penzance borough fire engine.**

Riot and Tumult

Newlyn, the dominant port in the South West, where eight million pounds worth of fish is landed in a year, has three layers of history. The old quay was built over 500 years ago, the main piers are a century old, and the new quay was opened by our present Queen in 1980.

Many a celebrated voyage has started here, from the epic to Australia by the lugger *The Mystery* in 1854 — it really was a mystery why she went — to the mission of the long-liner *Rosebud* to Parliament in 1937 in a bid to save fishermen's homes.

Newlyn was founded on the fishing industry, and will thrive as a 'living' village while this remains at its heart.

One of the fascinating chapters was written in May 1896. The regular glutting of the markets by the East Coast fishermen, with their 'Sunday caught' fish, brought a desperate situation. It was not altogether a religious conflict. It was a question of hard economics, with the local men, who kept Saturday and Sunday clear of fishing, having to demonstrate by force to make their point.

Right: **Before the building of the quays at Newlyn the fishermen, buyers and jowsters gather at the old pier, with the boats lying off in Gwavas Lake.**

It was a time, also, when the Newlyn School of Artists was enjoying great success. Gotch's *Alleluia* was bought by the Trustees of the Chantry Bequest for £900, and Forbes sold *The New Calf* for 1,000 guineas, during this month.

Mackerel were plentiful, prices were low. The impact of the Lowestoft boats, perhaps a couple of hundred of them, was enormous. One who remembered those days told me: 'I think that was the reason our young men went out of the villages. They never had enough to live on, and they couldn't face it.'

On this Monday morning of 18 May the local 'Sunday keep' fishermen of St Ives, Mousehole and Porthleven, joined with those of Newlyn, a heavy chain was fixed across the harbour and a 'boycott' enforced. It was estimated there were about 2,000 people on the pier. At Mousehole the 'baulks' were put down.

They boarded the visiting boats in the Newlyn harbour, intercepted others, and

Above: The story of the 12,000 mile voyage of the *Mystery* from Newlyn is the stuff of legend and heroes. Captain Richard Nicholls and his six colleagues sailed in this lugger in November 1854, and arrived at Melbourne, Australia, 116 days later, in March 1855. What a voyage! Times were hard enough at home, and there were stories of 'striking it rich' in the gold-fields Down Under, but there was no such fairy-tale ending. None made a fortune and many returned home. Their exploit is recorded on the plaque at the 'Ship Institute' at Newlyn, and I was present at this ceremony some thirty years ago, standing at the back on the left.

Right: The story of the *Rosebud*, one of West Cornwall's first battles for the environment, has long passed into folklore. This classic picture shows PZ 87 going up the Thames to the Houses of Parliament, bearing Newlyn fishermen and a petition asking the Government to save their homes.

over 100,000 mackerel were thrown overboard. 'No fish to be landed here today' was the notice they fixed on the pier, and those who disputed it were roughly handled.

Dozens of extra police were brought in, the magistrates came from Penzance, and the action of the Harbour Master Mr William Oats Strick in going out to warn approaching East Coast boats was so resented that a new notice went up: 'New harbour master or no more dues. One and All.' He was told: 'You have sold the Town.'

There were ugly scenes of violence when the fishermen marched on Penzance harbour armed with sticks and stones. The police drew their batons and charged.

Several people were badly hurt, there was damage on shore, and the authorities over-reacted so strongly that on the Wednesday over 300 men of the Royal Berkshire Regiment arrived by train, with rifles and ammunition. The red-coated troops marched to the old serpentine works at Wherrytown, and later — after another scuffle between the men of the two ports — marched to Newlyn, cleared the piers of people and removed the chain. The local men lined the streets and shook their fists — and the Lowestoft boats moved to Penzance.

These episodes were the start of deep

The 'Newlyn Riots' of May 1896 are a rich part of the history of West Cornwall fishermen. Sunday fishing by the visiting 'East Country' boats spoiled the markets for the local 'Sunday keeps', and times were lean enough anyway. The fishermen of Newlyn and Mousehole, together with those of Porthleven and St Ives — hundreds of them — took action on that celebrated Monday. Here, in these classic photographs, the soldiers of the Royal Berkshire Regiment arrive. They were put up at the old serpentine works, near the promenade, and marched on Newlyn.
Right: **Mr William James Bazeley, when he was Mayor of Penzance (1895–6) at the time of the 'Newlyn Riots'.**

hostility between the two towns. At that time they were not members of the same borough. For years many people refused to shop at Penzance . . . for did not this town council offer the East Countrymen the facilities of Penzance harbour for the rest of the season, and protection!

Newlyn fishermen asked the Home Secretary to receive a deputation to state their grievances, there were 'Questions in the House', and he was also asked to give assurances that measures would be taken to secure the conviction of the ringleaders.

'We are not rioters,' declared the Newlyn men. 'We did not require the police or the military. We are quiet and respectable men and those sent against us at Penzance are Sabbath breakers and drunkards.

'We are told by local gentlemen to go and do the same as the Lowestoft fishermen, which means to give up the privileges which our forefathers left us, to pull down the chapels and churches, take to the public house, and be a sabbath breaking people, with all the attending evils. We cannot do this.

'Die we may through starvation or other cause, but give up what has been the brightest and best part of our lives, Never!'

In another statement they put their case: 'The unwritten law or custom of this port is that everyone shall stop fishing from Friday night 'till Monday night so that markets may have a chance to clear themselves, and the fish are then in a better condition and prices are kept up through the whole week.

'What has irritated us is that the Lowestoft fishermen have made a statement that they will have our harbour, have our homes, and that they will take our wives. That is their fond boast.

'We are not fighting an isolated case. The Irishmen, the Scotchmen, and the Cornishmen all desist from fishing on

A pony and trap on Paul Hill at Newlyn, with a couple of cows and a calf going to market further down. The orchard on the right is now Kenstella Road.

Sunday. Lowestoft and Yarmouth are the only two ports that we are fighting. It is not the United Kingdom but these two places which are destroying our livelihood.'

Tempers cooled in a few days, the majority of the soldiers left within a week. During this time four destroyers had anchored in Mount's Bay.

It had been so serious that Newlyn Gala at Whit Week was postponed owing to 'recent events'! But it was so civilised that the Regiment played Penzance at cricket, and lost by 89 to 73 runs.

The sequel came with a number of fishermen of Newlyn charged with riotous assembly, and that they had made 'a great noise, riot, tumult, and disturbance'. Some were arrested in the Penzance court, having gone to give evidence in defence of others. In all nine were committed for trial at Bodmin.

Four of them were charged with assaulting the skipper of *The Warrior* — all pleaded not guilty. The Assizes trial was held on a Saturday, it went on into the night with William Triggs a central figure, and all stated in defence that they took no part in the disturbance.

It was 'Riot and Tumult' at Newlyn that Monday, said Mr Justice Lawrence, but on the second day of the trial there was a general collapse of the proceedings, with changes of plea. 'It was evident that an arrangement had been come to', during the week-end, was the contemporary comment.

They all had excellent characters, a lenient view was taken, and they were bound over to keep the peace for twelve months, even Mr Triggs. 'Don't go and say that I have sympathised with you. Don't go and say that because no punishment has been passed on you that no punishment was due', said the Judge. He hoped they would help bring peace back to Newlyn, and that they would justify his leniency. 'Thank you very much indeed, I cannot express my feelings towards you', said Mr Triggs.

There was bunting, and an enthusiastic welcome at Newlyn for the 'heroes', but the champions went to their homes with no great desire to be lionised. There was a bonfire on Mousehole Island, and bands played at Newlyn.

Did it all help keep the Sabbath? That was a question I once put to Mr Richard Cattran, who remembered the riot days and rifle tripods on the quay when he was a lad of seven.

'It helped partially, because those that didn't want to go to sea on Sundays put up a star flag on the mizzen mast — they were "Sunday Keeps". I think there were quite a few, and it lasted for a while, but eventually it died away,' he said.

Newlyn harbour in the 1890s, soon after the opening of the new North pier.

Above: It is 'E' for the good ship *Junior Endeavour* at the old Newlyn chapel in Boase Street, with the young Reverend Albert Pearson on the left in the pulpit. Pictured around 1917.
Left: It is Gala Day for the children of the Newlyn Methodist Sunday School — 'the Prims' — before the building of the road along from the bottom of the Slip. On Whit Monday they all marched to Trereife.
Below: Serious flooding at Newlyn Coombe and bridge at the turn of the century.

Above: Here is the Marazion Town Band in 1936.

Below: An exciting day for Fore Street, Marazion in 1905 when this traction engine (Fowler Imperatrix) went astray!

Above: A familiar name in Marazion down the century. Henry Reynolds — 'wool bought here' — had his butcher's shop at Marazion, in 1915.

Below: All smiles, these youngsters of Marazion Wesleyan Sunday School in 1910 at their tea treat on Treglowns picnic grounds.

Pride in its Past

Helston was a market town in King Alfred's time, for its Charter dates from 1201, the oldest in West Cornwall.

And what we can describe as its 'first-ever supermarket' is now the town's pride as a Folk Museum. The 1837 Market House is filled with treasures that not only reflect the distinctive history of the district, but demonstrate just how important it is to retain and display them. If only others would follow this example with such imagination.

This is the place where butter and eggs and meat were sold by farmers and their wives from the Lizard peninsula to the hungry miners of the Wheal Vor at Carleen. In the nineteenth century this was one of the largest mines in the world,

producing one-fifth of the total tin output. It covered four square miles with 1,400 men at work, Mr Martin Matthews recalled.

As Museums Officer here for the Kerrier District Council — working under Leisure Services manager Mr Roger Luke — he has a detailed knowledge of the Folk Museum, strengthened by a great personal interest as president of Porthleven Old Cornwall Society.

There is a fascinating display, large and small. The Furry Dance clock which plays that famous tune every half-hour, with ladies and gentlemen dancing in and out of the archways. The horse collar which hung for 60 years over the door at Rodda's saddlery in Church Street. The Cornish kitchen with its 'slab', the little old-fashioned shop, and the cobbler's workbench.

Dominating the scene is the 5½-ton wooden cider press of 1750, from Trelowarren. It took seventeen men to move it at the museum, and one recent photographing visitor turned out to be Mr Bulmer himself, from Herefordshire's famous firm that bears this name.

There is the model mine-stamp in action 'hammering' the rock to powder, the Smithy with the busy blacksmith, the charming wagonette from the Bosahan estate, and that impressive Godolphin family crest with its motto — in Cornish and not Latin — 'FRANK HA LEAL ETTO GE', which means Free and Loyal Thou Art.

In his small office,with its seventeenth

Left: **Outside the Angel Hotel in Helston's main Coinagehall Street: the road surface is in better condition today!**
Below: **An everyday scene at Meneage Street, Helston.**

century leaded glass window from a former Meneage Street bakery, Mr Matthews told me how the Museum had developed from those early days in the 1930s in the Corn Exchange by the Helston OCS. Their vigilance, the borough's support, the dedication of Mr Bill Dalton — who ran the Beehive Inn opposite — saw it grow. Kerrier have built mightily on these achievements.

'It has progressed so much that in March 1985 a "Friends of the Museum" group was formed with Mr Renfree Bray as chairman and Mrs Janet Godding as secretary', he told me. 'For there is concern for the future as well as great interest in the past. I want to encourage schools to take a keen interest in the Museum, and we plan exhibitions through the summer months to keep the interest of local people high.

'Now the worry is that we are running out of space. It may be we shall have to think of expanding to the rooms above.'

The parish bier, used at Mawgan for the old-time 'walking' funerals — in those days the mourners would walk from church to graveside singing hymns as they went — is on display. On top is the black coffin box kept in the Helston Union, the 'workhouse', and borrowed in emergencies by undertakers until a properly measured one was made. 'But that was in 1910 and you couldn't use it today because people have got so much taller,' remarked Mr Matthews.

'Almost every week some new exhibit is brought in. One of my favourites is the

Helston Folk Museum

***Above*: Rodda's Smithery was as much a part of Penzance as the Market House for many years! Second from left in this group of men is Mr Eddie Rodda, who still lives in Penzance.**

magnificent set of Imperial Measures used by the borough officers to check on the correct volumes of corn — the peck, the bushel and the gallon — as well as the scales to weigh the butter and meat, and the solid brass yardstick to measure the hides for the tanneries. For in those years the district had a large number of these, and local industry needed the strong leather thigh-boots and the working boots and shoes from the "cordwainers".

'One of the most exciting for me is the part dinner service, made from clay mined at Tregonning Hill for William Argal, the manager who kept the brick-making industry alive here. People were so grateful that on his retirement they presented a wonderful service with its blue floral design.'

***Below:* Humphry Millet Grylls, a Helston solicitor, helped to keep the famed Wheal Vor mine from financial disaster in 1830, and when he died £300 was subscribed to build this 'Monument' to his memory.**

Above: Everybody had their time cut out at Marazion, with St Michael's Mount in the background, lifting the 'earlies' in the 1930s. One man 'shakes the stems', another picks them up and puts them on one side, and the third double-checks that none are missed. A horse and plough would lead the way and a special feature shown here is the use of barrels for the potatoes. Mr Charles Tregoning of Gulval tells me that these held 96-lbs, and were mainly sent to the northern markets of Liverpool and Sheffield.

Below: New potatoes, the first of the season, all similar in taste, size and kidney-shaped . . . just perfect for the table. These were probably the May Queen variety, a thing of the past, harvested by hand at Gulval. You had to have the right hat for this job in those years.

It is 'croust' time on the farm and the men take a break. The threshing here, possibly in the St Buryan area, was carried out by the 'Marshall' steam engine, which was pulled by horses, before the advent of the traction engine. The steam engine would drive the 'thresher', and here the sheaves at the top are fed in. The loose straw would go up the 'lifter' — or elevator — to be stacked. The grain would go into the sacks. In the forefront above is Mr Ned Berryman, who lived at Ludgvan, 'the boss' who would go from farm to farm, at harvest time.

Above: The horse-drawn bus for the Poldhu Hotel waits at the railway station, with the GWR motorbus behind.

Below: The First and Last Inn at Alverton, Penzance, and the little donkey shay passes the St Just — Pendeen coach.

Above: The Land's End horse bus is just leaving Penzance: with a full load up! It may well be a wedding party on their way for a celebration trip with a visit to Logan Rock included

Below: No wonder they all stopped to look — one of the earliest motor cars at Penzance, around 1898, with chain drive and 'tiller' steering.

Defending the West

Mullion was not always a peaceful Cornish cove. It was a busy airship station during the First World War. 'It was in a wonderful position to counteract the German submarines which were working hard at that time to sink convoys coming in from the Western Approaches', said Mr John Owner who flew in many of these airships.

Up to 15 of them would go out together and search the area. Sometimes 24 would be out each day getting rid of submarines. 'There is not the slightest doubt it hastened the end of the war. These were non-rigid SS2 airships, 36 feet long, and did 65 miles an hour.

'We would go out over the sea, look down and drop a bomb on them. The Mullion station killed possibly 158 subs in a year, and I killed at least eight while I was there as pilot and observer.

'In the dark we were perfectly all right, and would often creep up on the subs, and they wouldn't know anything about it until they heard our bomb go bang. We could carry two large bombs of 100 pounds each, and one of 200 pounds . . . the pilot dropped the bomb.'

Mr Owner, who later came to live at Penzance, and became a member of the Town Council, continued with the airships until the end of the war.

Above: St Ives had its Volunteer Infantry Regiment in the days of the Napoleonic Wars, but here we see the volunteers of the town preparing to leave to serve King and Country in World War I.
Below left: Everybody lends a hand at the Eastern Green, digging tank traps in 1939 in case of invasion. Among the men is the local MP (in shirt sleeves, centre) Mr Alec Beechman, with pick.

Below: The trophies in front and the dominant gun must mean that these were top-rate marksmen. This group, in the late 1940s or early 1950s, with six-inch coast defence gun, are members of a Battery of 409 Coast Regiment, Royal Artillery at Penzance drill hall.

A Generation Short

The Cornish Exile longs to return home. Thousands of miles, and generations, may separate them from their 'roots', but the lure is magnetic and magical.

In few places is this more clear than at St Just at Feast week-end, when winter gives a November warning. No town in West Cornwall lost more of its sons and daughters, as Mr Jack Kevern, who lived at Cape Cornwall Street, told me.

'In 1861 the population was 9,140 against that of Penzance which was about 200 more. The last census showed St Just at 3,600. On one occasion 300 people left for Australia on one day. They left in September and arrived at Adelaide in January — with the number increasing by one on the journey,' he remarked.

There had been talk in brighter days of building a harbour at Cape Cornwall, to bring in fuel and take out tin, and of bringing the railway to town. They were not to be.

Because of the 'Great Emigration', where there is a hole in the ground you will find a Cornishman. They even say that when Pirie arrived at the North Pole he found a Cornishman there sinking a shaft!

One of my richest memories is of the end of a dinner-party in Springs, near Johannesburg. At the next table was a group of mining engineers, and we joined in *Going Up Camborne Hill*, with gusto! For not only emigration, but the School of

John Rowe's shop is now a house at Higher Bojewyan, but this scene has almost stood still down the years.

One of West Cornwall's most popular sports was hare coursing, and these men are ready to go.

Mines, has taken the Cornish tradition around the globe.

One day remains sharp in the history of the community, 20 October in 1919, when the Man-Engine broke at Levant, and 31 miners died. The old mine, started in 1820, had levels that went far out under the sea, one for more than a mile, and between 300–400 worked there.

The inquest verdict was: 'Accidental death caused by the breakage of a strap plate due to metal fatigue.' It was the only Man-Engine at work in Cornwall at this time, and the journey from top to bottom for the miner took about 25 minutes.

The names of the families bereaved rang of St Just history — Ellis and Trathen, Trembath and Tregear, Oats and Angwin and many more. It was 63 years later, on the anniversary in 1982, that a memorial plaque was unveiled in Trewellard Methodist Church, by a surviving widow.

The youngest survivor on that Monday was Mr Bill Lawry who told me some

***Above right*: Tragedy at the Levant mine, and the anxious wives and mothers wait for the news. Thirty-one miners died when the man-engine broke in October 1919.**
***Below:* Known as the 'Miners Parson', Reverend Barker Lumb is at Levant during those tragic hours. He helped the injured men, and gave great support to all who mourned.**

years ago of how the solars came down through the shaft. He was dug out fifteen hours later after falling 48 feet. 'My last memory was a blow on the head. The man riding below me and the man I had worked with, was found dead, and the man above me was dug out with his neck broken. He was on top of the rubbish that was covering me,' Mr Lawry remarked.

He had 36 stitches in his face and head, had a broken collar-bone, eight ribs crushed, and was home recovering for a year.

'I was the youngest one there, and I suppose I was the luckiest of the whole bunch because there was nobody above me that got out and the last man below me was killed. It was something I can never explain.'

I asked Mr Lawry what was his outstanding memory of the day. He replied: 'One thing that always struck me is that when the engine broke away everybody was singing one of the most wonderful hymns, and I can hear it almost now, *Lead Kindly Light*. 'I don't know if you have had the privilege of standing over a shaft and hearing the miners coming up singing, but it is out of this world.'

Mr Raymond Harry, then fifteen, was also one of the 'lucky ones' that day. He had reached the surface a half-minute before the tragedy. The man-engine was raising six men a minute and only three came up after him. 'We heard nothing — the engine dropped back eleven feet and shattered on itself,' he told me.

He returned to the mine when Levant reopened but thought it looked 'pretty ricketty and very precarious', and moved to Geevor. A year later, when everything shut down, he emigrated.

Mr Harry put it this way: 'The disaster at Levant put paid to St Just as my generation knew it. It will never be the same because hundreds of young people in my generation who left there, went to America, South Africa, Australia, Canada.

'Really, my generation is gone from there — there is a generation short in St Just,' he told me.

Below: **Mr Warren's 'The Star' at St Just, in Fore Street. The pub, and those 'mounting steps' so that customers could get on their horses without too much trouble, are still going strong.**

Left: In most mining pictures the 'Bal Maidens' are seen in their best attire. Here, with their bosses, they are in working clothes. Scores of these ladies were employed in the West Cornwall mines, on the surface, dressing the tin and copper ores. With their long-handled hammers they would carry out the work of 'spalling' or breaking-up the larger rocks, and then bringing them down to the size of walnuts . . . and a century ago being paid about one shilling a day. They worked in all weathers, and had a reputation for tough language and repartee. They had their own peculiar headdress, known in some districts as 'a yard of cardboard'.

Below: Geese were always part of the picture at Trewellard: flocks of them wandered about. The chapel is on the right with the road leading down to Levant mine.

Below: Pendeen Sunday School parade with the banner — still in the parish church — held aloft. On the left is The Radjel, on the right Carn View Terrace, and the Midsummer Day celebration is led by that remarkable personality, Reverend Barker Lumb, Vicar here from 1905 for almost 40 years.

Below: The band plays, the children wear the costumes and carry the banners of Wales and Scotland as well as fly the Union Jack in the Square at St Just. Is it Empire Day?

Meet the boys' section of St Just town silver band: many of these will be well remembered.

Below: Another banner, this time of the Wesleyan Reform Sunday School at Carnyorth out for the annual 'treat'. Leading the way is Mr Henry Branwell, towards Trewellard.

Above: Now we are in the Plain-an-Gwarry at St Just, with the Bible Christian Sunday School banner aloft.

Below: Look at these splendid hats for Trewellard Wesleyan Band of Hope special day.

Above: **Reverend Barker Lumb of Pendeen, probably in the Vicarage grounds with donkey and ladies.**

Below: **The Reverend Barker Lumb again with the young men and ladies of his Confirmation Class.**

Reflected Glories

One of the popular fallacies about the artistic 'invasion' that began a century ago is that the painters became part of the local communities of Newlyn and St Ives.

No such thing! True, some lodged in the cottages and spent their time with their palettes and easels in the streets and on the piers, but they did not identify permanently with the people. Few went to sea, few — if any — went to the Methodist chapels, or married local girls.

Educated and independent, they formed their own society, enjoyed their own entertainments.

Almost all were only spectators of this rich quaintness, captivated by the light and the simplicity. They came, like the tourists, with the advent of the railway line through Cornwall, and left just as easily.

This photograph has been reproduced more than any other in Newlyn, in painting and reprint. It catches the atmosphere of those early years of this century, with the fishermen all turning towards the harbour and the sea, and the nets hang out a-drying on the 'palings', with the new south quay in the background.

Yet Newlyn and St Ives inspired them.

Curiously, although there has nationally been a 'revival' of interest in the late Victorian paintings of West Cornwall, to the locals the appeal has always been at a high level. Down the years there has been a pride in the 'foreigners' who brought fame and celebrity, but not an affinity.

Henry Martin, Thomas Gotch, Walter Langley — with his heartbreaking scenes of tragedy at sea — were the first to arrive at Newlyn in 1882, but Stanhope 'Daddy' Forbes, with his lilting voice, was the Master.

The classic painting *Fish Sale* was exhibited at the Royal Academy in 1885, and is still regarded as the epitome of the 'Newlyn School'. It was he said, 'the best picture I have painted.' He lived at Higher Faughan until his death, at 90, in 1947.

Just as he wrote of Newlyn 'every corner was a picture', so St Ives became a magnet for artists after James McNeil Whistler 'wintered' here in the mid-1880s.

Within a few years the St Ives Arts Club, still flourishing at Westcotts Quay, was formed, and Julius Olsson, Algernon Talmage and Adrian Stokes were to the forefront of those who brought it prominence.

At Lamorna the arrival of Samuel John Birch in 1902 — he later took the name of Lamorna Birch and stayed for the rest of his life — and later Harold and Laura Knight, and Alfred Munnings, ensured a place in local art history for this lovely valley.

In our own time there has been equal international acclaim. The potter Bernard Leach, and sculptor Dame Barbara Hepworth, had honours showered upon them for their unique gifts. Today the brilliance of Patrick Heron, Ken Symonds, Denis Mitchell, Terry Frost, and John Wells, illumine West Cornwall, as did Ben Nicholson, Bryan Wynter, Roger Hilton, Charles Simpson and Geoffrey Garnier.

Significantly there has been a development of 'home-grown' artistic talent, from the 'primitive' Alfred Wallis to the Cornish-inspired Peter Lanyon, and to those of our present era, Bryan Pearce, Jack Pender, Margo Maeckelberghe, and Michael Praed.

They have come from a direct line of Cornish genius that began with Harold Harvey in West Cornwall, who spanned the generations with his work which is again enjoying such great popularity.

Left: **Many a time I have wondered if the photographers copied the artists' grouping, and then realised that they captured the reality that the painters recalled in their studios. This is Plein-Air photography at Mousehole, a beautiful example, in 1890.**
Right: **The cobbled Church Street at Newlyn in 1910, an artist's dream.**

Right: Dame Laura Knight spent more than a decade in Cornwall, happy and successful years from 1907 to 1918. With her husband, Harold, they became an important part of the 'Newlyn School' tradition. Her studies of nudes caused controversy, and she is seen at work here on one of these in this rare photograph.

Below: Among the younger members of the St Ives Society of Artists, formed in 1927, was Borlase Smart, who had come to the town as a student fourteen years before. He had trained in Plymouth where he had his first public exhibition, and went on to become a central figure at St Ives, with a studio overlooking Porthmeor beach. The sea, and the landscape's structure, were two of his dominant themes, expressed here in this Land's End study which he is completing in 1935. He died in 1947.

John Miller, of Sancreed, a contemporary artist with a great reputation.

Above: This Mount's Bay scene of the 1870s was painted by Samuel Phillips Jackson (1830–1904).
Left: Filling up the pitchers at North Corner, Newlyn.
Below: The net is hauled at St Ives — both popular subjects for the artists.

Above: This captures the beauty of West Cornwall: Cape Cornwall in 1895.
Left: One man and his grand-daughter, down at Cape Cornwall.

In their summer attire the men and women of St Buryan with their Wesleyan Sunday School banner.

An autumn day at Lamorna.

Above: Here is a sturdy group of children at Zennor's Logan Rock.

Below: The old fisherman and his dog on the slip at Penberth Cove.

Above: Fishermen at Porthgwarra, generations ago, sit on their lobster pots and barrels, and enjoy the sun and a chat in the 1880s.

Below and right: A pretty girl and boats on the slipway at this beauty spot of Porthgwarra.

Above: **They're off! The great motor-bike race gets under way at Land's End, with the return leg to London of the popular Easter week-end trials.**

Left: Land's End in all its magnificence.
Right: Bugle, flag and staves with the Scouts and Scoutmaster of the Land's End Troop.

The Golden Thread

Launching the lifeboat at St Ives, always a spectacular sight. Here, in the old days, the men take the strain. The boat is the *Caroline Parsons*, the date between 1933–38 with Coxswain Tom Cocking (centre), who died in the tragedy of 1939.

There was thick fog when the *Glamorgan Coast*, a 2,084-ton steamer, was wrecked in September 1932 at Cape Cornwall. Much of her cargo was salvaged by the men of Sennen.

The hearts of the people of West Cornwall are with their lifeboatmen. They know, from searing experience, of the unquenchable spirit of bravery that has been demonstrated at Penlee, St Ives and Sennen down the generations.

No area in Britain can have offered such an example.

A golden thread weaves its way through this lifeboat history: the service of the local fishermen, whose natural and inborn genius in the storms is allied to a strength of spirit that has no equal.

While the fishing industry survives so too will this vigour and dedication.

The first lifeboat at St Ives was the *Hope* in 1840, and the first silver medal was awarded 25 years later. Down the years, in this century, the Cocking family name has shone like a beacon for the mariner in peril.

Coxswain Tom Cocking is in charge of the lifeboat today, and it was his grandfather who gave his life in 1939 when six of the others in the crew died. The *John and Sarah Eliza Stych* capsized three times before being swept ashore.

The previous year the *Caroline Parsons* was wrecked while rescuing the crew of the *SS. Alba*, and Coxswain Cocking received a silver medal of the RNLI and a gold Cross of Merit from the Hungarian Government. Eight others received bronze medals — but just six months after the presentations almost all were drowned.

One man survived the awful tragedy of January 1939, Mr William Freeman, then 36, and those four hours changed his life. He was in bed when the maroon sounded at 2 a.m. that Monday morning. A last-minute volunteer, a 'spare hand', it was his first trip on a motor lifeboat.

Mr Freeman told me his remarkable story at his home some years before he died. 'I went down and she was on top of the slip. Someone gave up their jacket and I had it.

'The weather was a whole gale west nor'west,' he said. On the first capsize four were thrown out, his brother-in-law John Thomas, Edgar Bassett, the Coxswain, and William Barber. They could just see the pier head light, but soon the anchor they had dropped parted. They were two-thirds of the way across the bay when the lifeboat capsized again while Richard Stevens was trying to handle-start the engine.

'That left me and Matthew Barber and Jack Cocking in her. With no engines we had no hope of picking up anyone. I went into the cockpit and hung on to the wheel and the gear handle wheel.

'When she got up pretty close to Godrevy she capsized again, and threw Matthew Barber and Jack Cocking out. It didn't seem any time after that until she landed on the rocks on her side and I stepped out of her.'

Mr Freeman 'hung on for dear life', as he put it, knowing from the memories of the previous year that the lifeboat would come ashore. He told me, 'St Ives was almost like a ghost town for a while.'

He never went 'afloat again' for

The broken steamer *Bessemer City* of New York which ran on the rocks near Pen Enys Point, St Ives, in November 1936. All 33 were rescued by the St Ives lifeboat in three trips, with the Master not leaving until the vessel had split in two. The lifeboat *Caroline Parsons* was wrecked in January 1938, in the first of the two St Ives disasters.

In those old days the First and Last at Sennen was the 'last hotel in England', and opposite stood this lovely old Cornish cross.

although he was a fisherman before the tragedy he was never able to go out in a boat, let alone a lifeboat, from that day. But his son became a fisherman, and Mr Freeman said of those gallant men, 'St Ives still remembers with pride.'

Before this sad day the lifeboats of St Ives had been launched on service 128 times, and had rescued 434 without losing a single member of the crew.

Mr Cocking, Coxswain since 1967, and holder of two Silver Medals of the RNLI, received in 1985 the Miss Maud Smith award for 'the bravest act of lifesaving', and the Bower award, for the rescue of the crews of the tug and a coaster the previous year.

Just as the Cocking family is linked in history with St Ives, so the Nicholas family will always be associated with the great lifeboat heritage of Sennen which guards the vicious waters off Land's End.

The first boat, rowed with six oars, came in 1853, and eleven years later Coxswain Matthew Nicholas was awarded the silver medal for the rescue of the only survivor of *The Devon* from the Brisons. Coxswain Henry Nicholas 1893–1911, Coxswain Thomas Henry Nicholas 1929–59, and 2nd Coxswain James Howard Nicholas, continued the tradition of fisherman and rescuer.

Today Coxswain Maurice Hutchens, and the *Diana White*, carry the torch of over 130 years. One of the greatest moments came in September 1981 with the rescue of the crew from the 500-ton Icelandic vessel *Tungufoss*, with silver medal to Coxswain Hutchens and bravery awards from the Icelandic Government.

Above: The magic of Sennen Cove is in this scene. The Capstan House and the slipway, the crabbers and, on the right, the wharf with the Pilchard 'Press'.

Right: Crabs and lobsters galore come ashore at Sennen where the pots are still laid and hauled by the local fishermen.

All were saved, the lifeboat approaching the ship twenty times 'with the Coxswain using great skill to prevent his lifeboat striking the ship as she heeled further and further'.

In more recent times the Sennen Cove boat searched for hours in vain for the four boys from Stoke Poges Middle School who were swept from rocks at the base of Land's End cliffs in May 1985.

Hayle had its own lifeboat from 1866 to 1920, with 95 lives saved during that time, but was closed chiefly because of the decline in the coastal trade from the port and the end of sailing ships.

The first boat was the result of a fund collected at Oxford University and the victors of that year's Boat Race named her the *Isis* — on the Isis. In 1869 the crew of the brig *Lizzie* was rescued from the Stones, near Godrevy.

In the Spring of 1985 I was at Penlee boathouse near Mousehole when the memorial garden to those eight who died

The Duke of Atholl, centre, chairman of the RNLI shakes hands with Sennen lifeboat Coxswain Maurice Hutchens, surrounded by crew, officials and supporters.

The French collier *Ornaist* went aground at Perranuthnoe, in 1929, and was broken up on the beach.

in the tragic loss of the *Solomon Browne* in December 1981 was dedicated by Chaplain Reverend Hugh Cadman.

The memories came flooding in, for day by day, during the weeks after this grim loss, I had reported this unique chapter in Cornish lifeboat history. The funerals and the special services, the visits of the Duke and Duchess of Kent, the courage of the widows and families, the overwhelming world-wide response to the disaster fund appeal.

I remember, as though it were just an hour ago, the scenes of flag-draped coffins borne by lifeboat colleagues, and those words sung clear and true by the men of Mousehole:

Sunset and Evening Star —
And one clear call for me
And let there be no moaning at
the bar when I set out to sea . . .

To the mother of Coxswain Trevelyan Richards went a posthumous Gold Medal, with posthumous bronze medals for all the other crew members.

A Penlee lifeboat was stationed here from 1913 until 1983 when the 52-foot Arun *Mabel Alice* came to Newlyn. But the story of the local boat had begun earlier in 1803, at Penzance, and included years at Newlyn from 1908–13.

Just a few years before the loss of the *Solomon Browne*, Coxswain Richards was awarded the bronze medal of the RNLI, with Thanks on Vellum to the crew.

There had been bad weather for a week before the launch on 25 January in 1975 to go to the aid of those on the 1,000-ton coaster *Lovat* which sank eighteen miles south-south-west of Mousehole Island. There were only two survivors out of a crew of thirteen, and the Penlee men picked up five bodies.

There was a 'rough passage' getting there, the Coxswain told me. 'Conditions were very bad — the wind was west nor'west about 40-knots, gusting up to 75, storm force eight to nine, and in heavy squalls to force ten.

It was a sad day with bodies being picked up from the water and liferaft.

He was very pleased at his medal award, but said to me: 'I am glad the crew were also recognised because they did very good work that morning.' It was 28 years before the *Lovat* service that Penlee had previously gained medals and certificates, with the brilliant work at the *Warspite* wreck, on Cudden Ledges.

Coxswain Ken Thomas of the *Mabel Alice* has already made a reputation as the new leader, continuing the service in our own time of such men as Frank Blewett (Coxswain 1920–47), Eddie Madron (1947–57) and Jack Worth (1957–70).

A group of Mousehole fishermen and youngsters, of 1909. Among those in the back row are Marric Blewett, Martin Trewavas, Ben Hill Wright, and lads Wilfred and Benjamin Pender. Among those in front are Theopholis Trewavas, Frank Maddern, Joe Hocking and William Henry Hosking.

Above: **Feeding time for the young jackdaws in the early days of the Mousehole bird hospital and sanctuary with those remarkable sisters, Dorothy (right) and 'Pog' Yglesias.**

Below: **A crowded harbour at Mousehole: it was said that around 1900, when this photograph was taken, you could walk right across the harbour from boat to boat.**

Left: The story of the rescue of the eight crew members of the famed battleship *Warspite* is a celebrated one in the history of Penlee lifeboat. Here we see the *Warspite* aground on the Cudden Ledges, near Prussia Cove, in April 1947, and the crew *(below left)* with their awards for their service. In his first service as Coxswain, Edwin Madron was awarded the RNLI silver medal, Mechanic Johnny Drew received a bronze medal, with vellums for the crew, pictured here with the Mayor Mr J.T. Trezise and branch secretary Mr Barrie Bennetts. I told this story fully in the book *Mount's Bay*, with the dramatic personal memories of Mr Drew.

Above: The crew of the Penlee lifeboat, with their Coxswain Ken Thomas (centre, standing), at the boathouse with the relief boat *Guy and Clare Hunter*.

Above: Little is left of this wrecked ship on the Porthleven shore.

Above: These members of the Volunteer Lifesaving Company are on exercise in the Land's End district at the turn of the century. They were kept busy by the numerous wrecks around the coastline.

Right: The Norwegian three-masted steel barque *Gunvor* went on the rocks near Black Head, in April 1912, but all the crew escaped by lowering a ladder over the bows and getting ashore.

Gibson

Acknowledgements

My thanks, for so much help in recent years:
Ben Batten, John Corin, Helston Museum and its Museums Officer Martin Matthews, Penzance Town Council (and Tony Claypole of Penlee House), John Peak (secretary of the Morrab Library), the Editor of *The Western Morning News*, the Editor and staff of *The Cornishman*, Helen Derrington, Dennis Scobey, Rene Nash, Tom Honey, Charles Tregoning, Major Simon Bolitho, Anthony Holman, John Farmer (Cornwall county librarian), Terry Knight (Local Studies Library, Redruth), Margaret E. Bazeley, and so many friends, past and present, who have told me of their experiences and memories.
Photographers: Sam Bennetts, Andrew and Paul Besley, Eddie and Reg Richards, George Waterhouse.
Let me also pay tribute to those fine Cornish photographers of the past, Garfield Hall, Harry Penhaul, Tom Roskrow and the Gibson Brothers.

Bibliography: a selection

Bossiney Publications including *Mount's Bay* (Douglas Williams), *The Book of Penzance* (Cyril Noall and Douglas Williams), *Newlyn Towners, Fishermen and Methodists* (Ben Batten), *Cornish Shipwrecks* (Richard Larn and Clive Carter), *Wreck and Rescue round the Cornish Coast* (Cyril Noall and Grahame Farr), *Penlee Lifeboat* (John Corin and Grahame Farr), *The Book of St Ives* (Cyril Noall), *Sennen Cove and its Lifeboat* (John Corin), *Cornish Seafarers* (A.K. Hamilton Jenkin), *Cornish Seines and Seiners* (Cyril Noall).

Other Bossiney Titles Include

MOUNT'S BAY
by Douglas Williams.
More than 120 old photographs of an area stretching from Land's End to the Lizard with perceptive text by one of Cornwall's most respected journalists.
'. . . a fascinating and exhaustive study . . . It is a guidebook, potted history, pictorial gallery of Cornish life – all these things and very much more.'
The Western Evening Herald

100 YEARS AROUND THE LIZARD
by Jean Stubbs. 150 old photographs.
A beautiful title, relating to a magical region of Cornwall, well illustrated, with text by the distinguished novelist living near Helston.
'. . . writes with the skills of a professional novelist, the knowledge which comes from living here, and the enthusiasm which an enquiring mind can develop.'
The Western Morning News

AROUND LAND'S END
Michael Williams explores the end and the beginning of Cornwall. Wrecks and legends, the Minack Theatre, Cable & Wireless, Penwith characters and customs, lighthouses and Lyonesse all feature. 90 photographs, many of them from Edwardian and Victorian times, help to tell the story.
'. . . a delightful stroll not only along the lanes but the legends of this celebrated area.' The Cornishman

100 YEARS ON BODMIN MOOR
by E.V. Thompson. 145 photographs.
A rich harvest of old photographs and picture postcards, reflecting life on the Moor for a century with perceptive text.
'. . . timely that such a publication and collection of photographs should appear now, as a record for all of those who have loved and been inspired by Bodmin Moor.' Sarah Foot, The Western Morning News

RIVERS OF CORNWALL
by Sarah Foot, 130 photographs, 45 in colour.
The author explores six great Cornish rivers: the Helford, the Fal, the Fowey, the Camel, the Lynher and the Tamar.
'. . . makes use of many colour illustrations as well as black and white and shows that whatever changes may have taken place in the river economics they remain places of quality and beauty, quintessentially Cornwall.' The Cornish Guardian

WESTCOUNTRY MYSTERIES
Introduced by Colin Wilson. 45 photographs and old drawings.
'The Westcountry isn't just a place of beauty . . . it is also a place for some curious mysteries . . . A team of authors have joined forces to re-examine and probe various yarns from the puzzling to the tragic . . . well-written and researched.'
James Belsey, Bristol Evening Post

SEA STORIES OF CORNWALL
by Ken Duxbury. 48 photographs.
'This is a tapestry of true tales', writes the author, 'by no means all of them disasters – which portray something of the spirit, the humour, the tragedy, and the enchantment, that is the lot of we who know the sea.'
'Ken is a sailor, and these stories are written with a close understanding and feel for the incidents.'
James Mildren, The Western Morning News

NORTH CORNWALL IN THE OLD DAYS
by Joan Rendell, 147 old photographs.
These pictures and Joan Rendell's perceptive text combine to give us many facets of a nostalgic way of North Cornish life, stretching from Newquay to the Cornwall/Devon border.
'This remarkable collection of pictures is a testimony to a people, a brave and uncomplaining race.'
Pamela Leeds, The Western Evening Herald

CASTLES OF CORNWALL
by Mary and Hal Price. 78 photographs and map.
St Catherine's Castle and Castle Dore both at Fowey, Restormel near Lostwithiel, St Mawes, Pendennis at Falmouth, St Michael's Mount, Tintagel, Launceston and Trematon near Saltash. Mary and Hal Price on this tour of Cornwall explore these nine castles.
'. . . a lavishly illustrated narrative that is both historically sound and written in a compelling and vivid style that carries the reader along from one drama to the next.' Pamela Leeds, The Western Evening Herald

PEOPLE & PLACES IN CORNWALL
by Michael Williams. 60 photographs
Featuring Sir John Betjeman, Marika Hanbury Tenison, Barbara Hepworth and seven other characters, all of whom contributed richly to the Cornish scene.
'Michael Williams writes about ten very different people . . . openly aware of the permanent power and attraction Cornwall held for them.'
The Western Morning News

Other Bossiney Titles Include

HEALING, HARMONY & HEALTH
by Barney Camfield

COASTLINE OF CORNWALL
by Ken Duxbury

MYSTERIES IN THE DEVON LANDSCAPE
by Hilary Wreford & Michael Williams

PEOPLE & PLACES IN DEVON
by Monica Wyatt

125 YEARS WITH THE WESTERN MORNING NEWS
by James Mildren

UNKNOWN BRISTOL
by Rosemary Clinch

DARTMOOR IN THE OLD DAYS
by James Mildren

CURIOSITIES OF SOMERSET
by Lornie Leete-Hodge

GHOSTS OF SOMERSET
by Peter Underwood

AROUND BUDE & STRATTON
by Joan Rendell

UNKNOWN SOMERSET
by Rosemary Clinch
& Michael Williams

SOMERSET IN THE OLD DAYS
by David Young

STRANGE SOMERSET STORIES
Introduced by David Foot

UNKNOWN DEVON
by Rosemary Anne Lauder, Michael Williams, Monica Wyatt

CORNISH CHURCHES
by Joan Rendell

SEA STORIES OF DEVON
Introduced by E.V. Thompson

LEGENDS OF SOMERSET
by Sally Jones

VIEWS OF OLD EXMOOR
by Rosemary Anne Lauder

UNKNOWN CORNWALL
by Michael Williams

THE CORNISH COUNTRYSIDE
by Sarah Foot

AROUND GLORIOUS DEVON
by David Young

ECCENTRICS IN CORNWALL
by June Lander

GHOSTS OF CORNWALL
by Peter Underwood

VIEWS OF OLD PLYMOUTH
by Sarah Foot

CORNWALL IN UPROAR
by David Mudd

CURIOSITIES OF CORNWALL
by Michael Williams

We shall be pleased to send you our catalogue giving full details of our growing list of titles for Devon, Cornwall and Somerset and forthcoming publications.

If you have difficulty in obtaining our titles, write direct to Bossiney Books, Land's End, St.Teath, Bodmin, Cornwall.